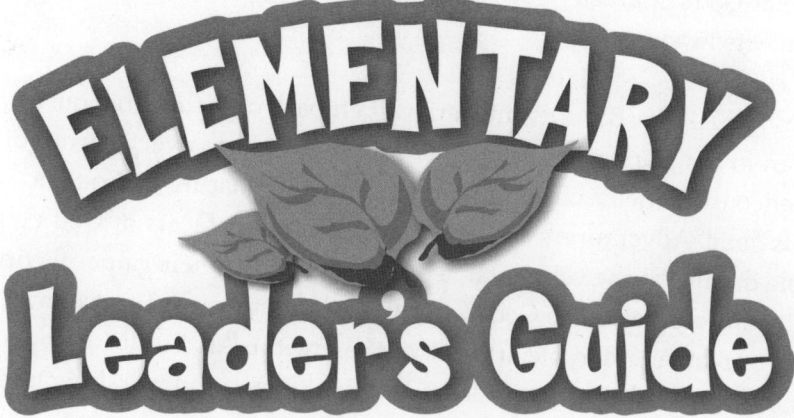

WILDWOOD FOREST VBS
ELEMENTARY LEADER'S GUIDE
Published by David C. Cook
4050 Lee Vance View
Colorado Springs, CO 80918 U.S.A.

David C. Cook Distribution Canada
55 Woodslee Avenue, Paris, Ontario, Canada N3L 3E5

David C. Cook U.K., Kingsway Communications
Eastbourne, East Sussex BN23 6NT, England

David C. Cook and the graphic circle C logo
are registered trademarks of Cook Communications Ministries.

ISBN 978-1-4347-6620-5

Cover Design: BMB Design
Interior Design: Sandy Flewelling (TrueBlue Design)
Interior Art: Aline Heiser
Photographs: Scot McDonald, Steve Starr
Videography: Revelation Films

Thanks to our gifted development team!
Rebekah Atkinson, Jeff Barnes, Shari Barr, MaryEllen Conaway, Cheryl Crews, Leigh Davidson, Bob de la Peña, Liz Duckworth,
Caroline Ferdinandsen, Diane Gardner, Cheri Gillard, Nancy L. Haskins, Jodi Hoch, Sharron Jackson, Dale Johnson, Patricia Keene, Dolores Kimball,
Kerry Krycho, Jessica Larrabee, Janet Lee, Tami Leonard, Douglas Mauss, Scot McDonald, Kevin Mullins, Brynn Paine, Karen Pickering,
Gail Rohlfing, Scott Stewart, Ed Stucky, Judi Tippie, Kelli Trujillo, Renée Gray Wilburn, Jill Williams, and Theresa With.

Printed in China

transforming lives together

Welcome to Wildwood Forest!

Your young Adventurers may know about God—but do they know who he really is? Wildwood Forest VBS is a place where children will discover that God's character goes beyond their imaginations—and can be revealed in exciting, unexpected ways.

In David C. Cook's 2009 VBS, Adventurers will embark on a thrilling journey into Wildwood Forest, an inviting and mysterious place of discovery. In every corner of this forest, children will encounter the fascinating, life-transforming nature of God and find that he is as wild as he is good. Adventurers will experience the many facets of God's character with hands-on Bible dramas at the Great Oak Theater, challenge their game-playing skills at VineLand Adventure Course, see God's power firsthand through fun experiments at Glow Rock Hideaway, create memorable artwork at the Treetop Art Studio, enjoy a time of refreshment and rest with the tasty snacks at Harvest Grove, and worship our amazing God at The Heights.

We've given you everything you need to make this incredible week easy to plan and manage. This guide provides helpful suggestions and materials to transform each Discovery Site into a fantastic, overgrown forest bursting with adventure and fun. Every activity children participate in is founded on biblical teaching, ensuring that this forest trek will change lives.

Each location Adventurers visit in the rotation comes with its own guide. Just follow the simple instructions in this guide and you're ready to go! Every guide is packed with options and suggestions for each day of this forest adventure. Whether you're leading children through games, snacks, Bible dramas, crafts, learning labs, or music and Bible memory, you'll have complete freedom to customize your Discovery Site to suit the unique needs of the children you lead through Wildwood Forest.

Every child has a special place in this forest, regardless of age. So in addition to this elementary guide, Adventurers in fourth and fifth grades can enjoy a more extreme journey through Wildwood Forest: Backcountry Trek. And preschoolers will join BOZ, the Green Bear Next Door™, on their adventure through the tamer areas of the forest in Wildwood Forest: BOZ's Great Adventure. These options give your church an opportunity to reach children at their own level. They'll enhance and optimize each Adventurer's experience. And you'll find they make VBS more manageable too!

Everything you need to get started is waiting for you in the pages ahead. So get ready for a week that will change lives, and prepare for a bold journey into Wildwood Forest—where kids and leaders alike discover the wild heart of God.

—The David C. Cook VBS Development Team

TABLE OF CONTENTS

Wildwood Forest Adventure Map: VBS Week Overview

	BIBLE STORY	KEY VERSE	LIVE IT!	GREAT OAK THEATER Bible Dramas	TREETOP ART STUDIO Crafts
Day 1	A Wild Battle—Gideon's Fight (Judges 7:1–8, 16–22)	1 Samuel 17:47 It is not by sword or spear that the LORD saves; for the battle is the LORD's.	God is undefeatable.	A man named Gideon discovers God's undefeatable power when his tiny army defeats an enemy thousands strong.	*Elimination Game* or *Wildwood Forest Yarn Magnets*
Day 2	A Wild Stand—The Fiery Furnace (Daniel 3:1–29)	Psalm 47:2 How awesome is the LORD Most High, the great King over all the earth!	God is unmatchable.	Three friends make a stand for the true God in spite of being threatened with death.	*Burnt Ropes Plaque* or *"The Forest Is Alive!" Puzzle*
Day 3	A Wild Rescue—Paul and Silas's Night in Prison (Acts 16:16–34)	Acts 16:31 "Believe in the Lord Jesus, and you will be saved."	God is uncontainable.	Paul and Silas are thrown into prison, but find that God's message can't be contained for long.	*"Jesus Frees" Key Holder* or *Pages of Praise*
Day 4	A Wild Encounter—Elijah Meets God in a Whisper (1 Kings 19:9–18)	Psalm 46:10 "Be still, and know that I am God."	God is unpredictable.	A prophet learns about God's unpredictable yet faithful nature when he climbs to a mountaintop and experiences a great wind, an earthquake, a fire, and a gentle whisper.	*Whisper Chimes* or *Leafy Mobiles*
Day 5	A Wild Love—The Birth of Jesus (Luke 2:1–20; Matthew 2:1–12)	1 John 4:14 And we have seen and testify that the Father has sent his Son to be the Savior of the world.	God is unforgettable.	An unforgettable Savior is born amidst amazing miracles and wondrous occurrences.	*Lamb of Love* or *Wildwood Forest Leaf Coasters*

VINELAND ADVENTURE COURSE: Games	HARVEST GROVE Snacks	THE HEIGHTS Bible Memory and Music	GLOW ROCK HIDEAWAY Learning Lab
Battle Tug Play a reverse tug-of-war game to collect the most "torches." **Smash and Dash** Try to knock down the opposing team's jars while protecting your own.	**Battle on the Bagel** or **Animals in the Forest**	**"The Battle Is the Lord's"** (Praise Music and Video) **Match Snatch** or **The Hula Spear-It** (Key Verse Memory Activities)	**Who's Got the Power?** Balloons flip and fly through the air, showcasing God's undefeatable power.
Walk the Plank Reverse the order of your team's line while standing on a 2" x 4" plank. **Fiery Furnace Friends** "Nebuchadnezzar" tries to tag other players, who are only safe when they are standing together.	**Stick Together Sundaes/ Sandwiches** or **Forest Flowers with Wildwood Dip**	**"How Awesome"** (Praise Music and Video) **Twist and Shout** or **Toss Across** (Key Verse Memory Activities)	**Find the Faker** A plastic bag explodes, revealing the fake experiments and teaching Adventurers about our unmatchable God.
Jailbreak Get to the opposite side of the field without getting tagged and taken to jail. **Outrageous Rescue** Free your team's prisoner by collecting and putting in order all six Bible story cards.	**Prison Bars** or **Sweet Trees**	**"Be Saved"** (Praise Music and Video) **Line by Line** or **Have a Ball!** (Key Verse Memory Activities)	**Let's Bust Out of This Joint** A tiny index card is transformed into a big hoop, showing that God is uncontainable.
Be Still Follow the directions on the game cube to get to the other side of the field. **God's Whisper** Toss as many team plates as possible into a box.	**Stop, Look, and Listen Mix (God Speaks!)** or **Tree Bark and Branches**	**"Be Still"** (Praise Music and Video) **Puzzle Power** or **Balloon Bog** (Key Verse Memory Activities)	**An Amazing Melting Mixture** An unpredictable mixture oozes and solidifies, teaching that God is also unpredictable.
Manger Madness Find the hidden star and return it to the sideline without getting tagged. **Unfolding Love** Create Bible story shapes with a tarp—without stepping off.	**Star Parfait** or **Ants and Ladybugs and Frogs on a Log**	**"The Unforgettable Savior"** (Praise Music and Video) **Stone Scripture Search** or **Fast Forest Frolic** (Key Verse Memory Activities)	**God's Light to the World** Various objects glow under a black light, reminding Adventurers that God is unforgettable.

Leading a Child to Christ

It's amazing how often adult Christians say that they first understood God's plan for salvation when they were between six and twelve years old. These years are key for children to make personal decisions for Christ and to begin their faith journeys. Wildwood Forest VBS may be the experience that inspires a child to express faith in Christ and receive God's saving grace.

Keep in mind that no two children are at the same point of spiritual preparedness. Many children aren't ready to trust in Christ even at the upper end of elementary school; other children can be quite sincere in saying they want Jesus to be their Savior even as preschoolers. They're sensitive to their need for forgiveness and acceptance into God's family. Be open to the Holy Spirit's leading. Be available to answer questions, but let children decide when the time is right to receive Christ. Here are a few tips:

Be careful not to let your eagerness spur children to make a faith decision, since VBS is a time when our radar is eagerly seeking kids who are ready to trust Christ for salvation. Kids will pick up on what will make the teacher happy and perhaps say they want to make a decision, when the truth is they don't yet understand what they're saying.

Find opportunities to invite children to receive Christ individually, rather than just making group invitations. Kids are great conformists; they may respond to such an invitation just because everyone else does. Encourage children to talk privately with you about questions regarding salvation and what Jesus wants to do in their lives, and then be available for these conversations.

Have the child use his own words to explain his decision. If you feel the child understands the concept of salvation and is ready to receive Christ by faith, take a few minutes to pray with him. You and the child will want to talk with parents about this decision. Parents who don't attend church may have questions about salvation, and this opens the door for you to tell them about Christ and invite them to your church.

Remember your important ministry of follow-up. Pray for the child and encourage discipleship and Christian growth. Send a personal note—kids love to get mail addressed to them!

Explaining Salvation

The following suggestions may be helpful as you explain the message of salvation. Help the child understand the truths that are fundamental for all Christians. Make copies of the reproducible on page 8 of this guide. It will help the child follow these important steps and give her something to take home as a reminder of her decision.

Step 1: God loves us even though we sin (Romans 5:8). We must recognize that we deserve God's punishment, and his love is a free gift (Romans 6:23).

Step 2: Even though God loves us, our sin separates us from him. But he wants to forgive us, and he will if we ask (1 John 1:9).

Step 3: Believing in Jesus, asking for his forgiveness, and inviting him to lead your life is the way to accept God's free gift (Romans 10:9–10). Jesus is God's perfect Son, and he died on a cross to take the consequences of our sin (John 3:16). But Jesus didn't stay dead. God brought him back to life to prove he's stronger than our sin. Because Jesus died and rose again, God will forgive us.

Step 4: Once we ask for God's forgiveness, we can celebrate because we're sure he forgives us (1 John 1:9). Now we're part of God's family forever (John 1:12), and we want to learn as much about him as we can. Reading the Bible, praying, and worshipping are some ways we learn more about him (2 Peter 3:18).

Step 5: When we have the good news of being in God's family (John 1:12), we want to tell others about it (Matthew 10:32; 28:19). Encourage children to express their decisions in their own words. Clarify any confusion.

During your conversation, you may want to share some additional verses with the child. The verses below might help. Read them from a Bible, not just the page. You don't have to use them all in every conversation. Choose the verses that answer the questions of individual children.

- *John 1:12*—"Yet to all who received him, to those who believed in his name, he gave the right to become children of God."

- *John 3:16*—"For God so loved the world that he gave his one and only Son, that whoever believes in him shall not perish but have eternal life."

- *Romans 3:23*—"For all have sinned and fall short of the glory of God."

- *Romans 5:8*—"But God demonstrates his own love for us in this: While we were still sinners, Christ died for us."

- *Romans 6:23*—"For the wages of sin is death, but the gift of God is eternal life in Christ Jesus our Lord."

- *Romans 10:9-10*—"If you confess with your mouth, 'Jesus is Lord,' and believe in your heart that God raised him from the dead, you will be saved. For it is with your heart that you believe and are justified, and it is with your mouth that you confess and are saved."

- *2 Corinthians 5:17*—"Therefore, if anyone is in Christ, he is a new creation; the old has gone, the new has come!"

- *1 John 5:11-12*—"And this is the testimony: God has given us eternal life, and this life is in his Son. He who has the Son has life; he who does not have the Son of God does not have life."

Discovering Jesus as Your Savior

1 God loves us, but he does not like our sin. The Bible teaches that all people have sinned or disobeyed God (Romans 3:23). *How have you sinned by disobeying God?*

2 The Bible says that our sin separates us from God (Romans 6:23). But God provides a way for us to be connected with him again so we can live with him forever. We need God's forgiveness. *Do you want to know how to be forgiven by God?*

3 Jesus is God's perfect Son. Jesus died on a cross to take the consequences for our sins (John 3:16). Because Jesus died for us, God forgives our sins. *Do you believe that Jesus died on the cross to forgive you of your sins?*

4 Jesus didn't stay dead. The Bible tells us that he rose from the dead and is alive today. So we can talk to him right now. If we believe that Jesus died on the cross to take the consequences for our sins (Romans 10:9–10), we can ask God to forgive us. The Bible promises that if we ask God to forgive us, he will (1 John 1:9). *Would you like to ask God to forgive you for your sins?*

5 Once we have asked Jesus to forgive us, our sins are forgiven. Jesus saves us from the result of our sins. When we trust Jesus as our Savior, we are part of God's family forever (1 John 5:11–12). Because we are part of his family, we are to live in ways that please God and do things that help us learn more about him (Colossians 1:10). *What are some ways you can learn more about Jesus?*

6 Now that you are forgiven and part of God's family (John 1:12), you will want to share your decision with others. *Who would you like to share your decision with?*

Survival Guide: Bible Story Summaries

Day 1 A Wild Battle

A Little Background...

Remember your childhood fears? Maybe it was a bogeyman in the closet, or maybe you were afraid of the dark. All children deal with fears about things both imaginary and real. Younger children (ages 0-6) can be afraid of a variety of things, such as being separated from their parents. But many of their fears can be about things that aren't real, like monsters and ghosts. Older children (ages 7-12) fear more realistic things. Death, violence, and natural disasters often scare them the most.[1]

We adults haven't outgrown fears; they just look a bit different now. We don't worry so much about imaginary monsters in the closet—real life has plenty of "monsters" that can keep us awake at night. Unpaid bills or financial worries, threats of terrorism and news of war, health problems and fears of diseases like cancer or Alzheimer's, crime, identity theft, and much, much more. And we tend to deal with our fears differently than children: teddy bears or blankets won't do the trick against worries like these. We turn to other more grown-up "solutions" like stressing out, overeating, lying awake and sleepless at night, becoming a workaholic, sending up occasional desperate prayers, or relying entirely on ourselves to solve the problem (and developing high blood pressure in the process!).

The reality is that fears can be paralyzing. When we face them, we can deal with them in two different ways. One way is to turn to human attempts to overcome them, either relying on ourselves or giving in to extreme worry and anxiety. The other approach is illustrated in today's Bible story: we can rely fully and completely on God! In Judges 7, Gideon's army faced a daunting task: defeating a massive army. But instead of mustering their courage, God purposefully made them vulnerable by reducing their number from 32,000 soldiers to just 300. God wanted his people to learn that he was their source of victory, so he put them in a terrifying position where they were, in essence, *forced* to trust solely in him. When the victory came about, there was no way they could take the credit for what happened—it would be crystal clear to them that God's power is what defeated the enemy.

The fact of the matter is that God is bigger and more powerful than *any* fearful situation or challenge we face. He cannot be defeated. His plans cannot be thwarted. Nothing can stop his will, his might, or his love. And this same God who defeated an army as numerous as the sand on the seashore is at your side, guiding your life. As you face the fears of life in this dangerous world, put your trust in him: the battles you face *are the Lord's*.

[1] This information about childhood fears can be found at http://kidshealth.org/parent/emotions/feelings/anxiety.html.

Bible Story
Gideon's Fight
(Judges 7:1–8, 16–22)

Key Verse
It is not by sword or spear that the LORD saves; for the battle is the LORD'S.
(1 Samuel 17:47)

Live It!
God is undefeatable.

Day 2 *A Wild Stand*

Bible Story
The Fiery Furnace
(Daniel 3:1–29)

Key Verse
How awesome is the LORD Most High, the great King over all the earth! (Psalm 47:2)

Live It!
God is unmatchable.

A Little Background...

Remember high school English class when you learned to diagram a plot? There was the beginning and the end, but the key was identifying the story's *climax*— the moment of tension, the moment of decision. It's that time in the story when you don't know what will happen next and you're hanging on the writer's every word.

So here's the question: What's the climax of today's Bible story? You may automatically assume that it's the moment of the miracle: when the fourth man appears in the fiery furnace and Shadrach, Meshach, and Abednego are supernaturally protected from injury and death.

But perhaps the true climax is a few verses earlier, in Daniel 3:16–18. After refusing to bow down and worship an idol, these three friends bravely assert their belief in God's power to save them. And here's the real clincher: they say, "But even if he does not, we want you to know, O king, that we will not serve your gods or worship the image of gold you have set up" (3:18). These young men don't yet know the end of the story. They haven't been promised a miracle or a dramatic rescue. They fully realize that God may let them be executed—but they don't care. They will not, under any circumstances, worship anyone or anything other than the true God.

That amazing moment in the furnace? That's more the compelling conclusion to the story. The true climax is the dramatic leap of faith—the tenacious declaration to worship only the real God.

You won't face a fiery furnace in your life, but you certainly face daily moments in which the choice is yours: bow down to the idols of our culture, or worship God alone, despite the consequences. There may be a price you have to pay, but as Shadrach, Meshach, and Abednego knew, the cost is worth it when you've got an opportunity to stand boldly for the one true God.

The true climax comes in the moment of choice. Today, choose to stand for our unmatchable God.

Day 3 *A Wild Rescue*

Bible Story
Paul and Silas's Night in Prison (Acts 16:16–34)

Key Verse
"Believe in the Lord Jesus, and you will be saved." (Acts 16:31)

Live It!
God is uncontainable.

A Little Background...

"The best laid schemes o' mice an' men ..."

These words, penned by the Scottish poet Robert Burns, speak aptly to today's story: the best-laid plans of humans often go awry ... *especially* when those humans are aiming to disrupt *God's* plan!

When Paul and Silas ruined the moneymaking scheme of some slave owners, they were beaten and imprisoned. The ultimate goal was to shut them up— to keep them quiet about Jesus and to silence the life-changing message they were preaching. But there was one tiny problem: no matter how many chains they put on Paul and Silas, there was no way they could come up with a scheme that would stop God.

That night when Paul and Silas worshipped God, the other prisoners heard their songs and prayers. And they experienced God's power for themselves as their chains fell off. Then the prison guard and his entire family enthusiastically committed their lives to Jesus!

God's message, God's power, and God's purposes are uncontainable, unstoppable, irrepressible, and inescapable. The gospel, quite simply, cannot be chained up. It's the "power of God for the salvation of everyone who believes" (Romans 1:16)!

How have you experienced the persistent, unstoppable, uncontainable love and power of God in your own life? When have circumstances attempted to keep you from God's love or God's truth? And how did God break through? Take a moment right now to praise God for that experience and to worship him for his uncontainable power and love.

Day 4 A Wild Encounter

A Little Background...

There's no shortage of examples of God revealing himself in powerful and mighty ways in Scripture. God used a pillar of fire to guide the Israelites (Exodus 13:21); God made the sun stand still (Joshua 10:13); God's presence caused Mount Sinai to look like a volcano (Exodus 24:15-17); Jesus' appearance became blindingly brilliant in the transfiguration (Matthew 17:2); and Jesus calmed a raging storm (Luke 8:24).

Elijah himself had *just* witnessed one of the most memorable examples of God's mighty power in Scripture. In a face-off with 450 prophets of Baal, Elijah showed tenacious faith as he called down fire from heaven. And God showed up in an awesome way, consuming Elijah's offering in a blaze of hungry flames (1 Kings 18).

Elijah had experienced God's awesome, powerful presence. But *this* time, in today's Bible story, God had something else in store for Elijah—something surprising, unexpected, and unpredictable. God came to Elijah in a still, quiet whisper.

The point for Elijah—and for us—is certainly *not* that God only reveals himself in quietness and not in displays of power. After all, God clearly has used tremendous acts of nature (like the windstorm, the earthquake, and the fire) in Scripture to reveal his presence or bring about his will.

The point is that God isn't *limited* to those things. God isn't only big, powerful, and awesome. God is also beautiful, true, peaceful, and good. God cannot be squished into our box; God isn't defined by our human constructs or by

Bible Story
Elijah Meets God in a Whisper
(1 Kings 19:9–18)

Key Verse
"Be still, and know that I am God." (Psalm 46:10)

Live It!
God is unpredictable.

manmade notions. God is *God* … and God's nature is unpredictable, amazing, and often wildly surprising.

Just as God revealed his presence to Elijah, God is present with you daily if you have a faith relationship with him. And just as God surprised Elijah, God may reveal himself to you in surprising ways. Maybe he'll speak to you through a thunderstorm or a lightning flash or a blazing sunrise. Or maybe it will be through a sense of direction you feel during a time of prayer. Or maybe it will be through the encouraging words of a friend or a Bible verse that hits you right in the heart. Seek God expectantly. And get ready to be surprised!

Day 5 A Wild Love

A Little Background...

Incarnation.

It's a big word with an even bigger meaning. At its core, it means "enfleshed." It's the theological terminology that sums up the mystery of that night in Bethlehem, when the God who spins both planets and electrons in orbit was birthed as a helpless, crying infant. It's the paradox of the King of all creation resting in a cradle of straw.

John uses powerful imagery to hint at the meaning of the incarnation. He writes, "The Word became flesh and made his dwelling among us" (John 1:14). It's a word picture that would've brought a visual image to mind immediately for the first-century reader: the image of a tent being pitched among other tents and dwelling places. It's the idea that God isn't far off—he's *here*. By taking on flesh, God has come to us … is with us … is among us … is one of us.

Today's Bible story contains many unforgettable moments: Mary and Joseph turned away from an overcrowded inn, the sky filled with singing angels, shepherds arriving to worship the baby in the manger. But the greatest miracle—the most unforgettable—is the quiet one. It's the miracle without drama or lights or song. It's the miracle of Jesus' very existence, both fully God and fully human.

From the moment of his birth, Jesus was headed toward the cross, because he was born for a purpose: to save the world. As a man three decades later, Jesus would suffer and die on the cross to pay the penalty for our sin (Romans 6:23). And he would rise from the dead three days later to show his victory over that sin. Through belief in him, we can be saved.

And through that salvation, we can have a *relationship* with him. He isn't a God somewhere out there, far off and distant from everyday life. He's the God who came here, who breathed and laughed and hurt. He's the God who dwelt among us, in the flesh. He's the God who chose a manger as his first cradle … because he loved us.

Bible Story
The Birth of Jesus
(Luke 2:1–20;
Matthew 2:1–12)

Key Verse
And we have seen and testify that the Father has sent his Son to be the Savior of the world. (1 John 4:14)

Live It!
God is unforgettable.

Wildwood Forest: Elementary Program Overview

Welcome to Wildwood Forest Vacation Bible School! In Wildwood Forest, children discover the untamed nature of God. As they encounter His undefeatable, unmatchable, uncontainable, unpredictable, and unforgettable character, their lives can be transformed. This book will guide you through creating a memorable VBS experience for elementary-aged children.

Begin by looking through the *Wildwood Forest Director's Guide* to get an overall picture of the entire Wildwood Forest program. Then, turn to this guide to help you oversee your portion of Wildwood Forest. Here, you'll find information on the opening and closing assemblies, an overview of how the elementary program works, and simple instructions on getting volunteers started on the various Discovery Sites are included. So with this guide in hand, get ready to set off on an adventure!

QUICK TIP!
Separate all-in-one guides are available for the preschool and upper elementary age levels. Although separate programs for children in these age groups are not required, they can heighten the impact of your program.

Organizing and Running Wildwood Forest VBS

You'll find you can run the Wildwood Forest elementary program simply and effectively. This guide provides the resources you'll require to oversee the elementary program as a whole and to organize the opening and closing assemblies. You'll also need the six site guides included in the Wildwood Forest VBS Starter Kit. These site guides contain complete information on running each Discovery Site in Wildwood Forest (such as crafts or snacks). Simply hand these resources to your volunteers and let them take it from here.

The six guides are:
Harvest Grove Snack Guide,
Treetop Art Studio Craft Guide,
Glow Rock Hideaway Lab Guide,
Great Oak Theater Drama Guide,
The Heights Bible Memory and Music Guide,
and VineLand Adventure Course Games Guide.

You may have been asked to oversee the registration and logistical organization of the Wildwood Forest elementary program. If so, the *Wildwood Forest Director's Guide* provides further information on planning, recruiting, and post-VBS follow-up. It will also guide you step-by-step, offering ways to group children, move them from Discovery Site to Discovery Site, and arrange the activities within your church's physical space.

QUICK TIP!
Plan on having one Explorer or Scout for every six to eight children in younger grades, and one for every eight to ten children in older grades.

QUICK TIP!
For site-based instructions, see page 91 in the *Wildwood Forest Director's Guide.*

QUICK TIP!
Wildwood Forest VBS is easy to staff! You need five leaders—one per Discovery Site. We recommend a helper for each Discovery Site as well. Then, recruit five more helpers to lead the five groups of children through the forest. Leaders and helpers can double up in many places—for example, taking roles in the opening or closing assembly.

Key Players

A team of volunteers will make your Wildwood Forest VBS a reality! Staffing needs are explained in detail in the *Wildwood Forest Director's Guide* beginning on page 63, but keep these key players in mind as you learn about running Wildwood Forest.

Discovery Site Leaders: Plan on one adult leader to organize and run each Discovery Site.

Explorers and Scouts: Plan on at least one Explorer or one Scout for each color-coded group of children. These are adults or teens who want to help without any preparation. You may also want to assign an Explorer or Scout to each Discovery Site to assist with preparation and help everything run smoothly.

Actors: For the opening assemblies, you'll need one person to serve as the emcee, who we're calling Ranger Riley, and three adults or teens to serve as actors.

Rotational Model

Wildwood Forest VBS is built on a rotational model. This means the Adventurers will be divided into groups, and each group will rotate to—or visit—every activity at Wildwood Forest every day. All the children start together at the opening assembly. Then they divide into five groups and rotate through five activities: Bible drama, Bible memory and music, crafts, games, and lab. Each group visits all five Discovery Sites each day, but in a different order. With each group beginning at a different starting point, the groups rotate through the Discovery Sites. All the groups take a break and visit Harvest Grove together for refreshments halfway through. In a rotational model, the children move and the teachers stay put. Picture a circle with groups arranged around the rim. As the circle turns, the groups move until they have been all the way around. For more information on grouping children, see page 25 in the *Wildwood Forest Director's Guide.*

Moving Children around Wildwood Forest VBS

Moving your Adventurers around your church's Wildwood Forest VBS is easy to do. You or the VBS Director will assign every Adventurer to a color-coded group, and give each a bandanna of the assigned color (labeled with each child's name). Have Explorers and Scouts wear T-shirt colors that match their group. Be sure that Explorers and Scouts get to know their assigned children.

Explorers and Scouts will lead their groups to every Discovery Site. There they stay close by (not watching from the sidelines!) and participate in the activities. While moving their assigned groups between Discovery Sites, they should keep the children in line and on task. The Adventurers don't even have to know their way around; the Explorers and Scouts will take them safely to the next site.

Keeping it All Together

Every day Adventurers will have "stuff" to carry around with them, such as backpacks, purses, or a sweater for a chilly morning. As the day moves along, Adventurers will naturally shed these things and be reluctant to carry them around. In addition, each child will have a craft and a student book that will travel with them through Wildwood Forest.

To keep all these things together, give Explorers and Scouts laundry baskets (matching their group's color, if possible), a tote, or a box to carry with them as they lead their group around Wildwood Forest VBS. Adventurers can store their items in the basket to keep from getting loaded down or losing things. Everything will then be conveniently on hand if someone needs something. You'll also want to provide each leader with markers to identify individuals' student books and craft items.

You'll be glad you made the investment in several inexpensive laundry baskets or bins when you come to the end of each day and all the children have their things—without stress!

Options, Options, Options...

You will find numerous options throughout Wildwood Forest VBS, from various craft, snack, and game choices to local mission project ideas to dozens of **Climb Higher** opportunities. You and your staff have the freedom to create a VBS experience that fits the unique needs of your children, church, and community. As you read through the guides, remember that you each may or may not choose to implement every idea and suggestion given. And rather than be overwhelmed by the variety of options presented, be flexible; do what works for your program, and remember to have fun!

Handy Resources

As you and your volunteers plan the details of each Discovery Site for your VBS, keep these resources in mind.

- **Music and music video:** "Wild and Wonderful God" is this year's theme song. Find the music on the *Wildwood Forest Praise Songs* CD and on the *Wildwood Forest Music and Promo* DVD as a music video with motions. Choose either way to open each day's program. Use this music as you choose—in your opening each day, as background music for any Discovery Site, or in your closing assembly. Music and lyrics for all ten Wildwood Forest songs can be found on the *Wildwood Forest Program Resources* CD-ROM.
- **Reproducible artwork:** Clip art is available on the VBS Web site (www.davidccook.com/vbs), and on the *Wildwood Forest Promotional Materials* CD-ROM. You can use this artwork to create a mysterious forest,

QUICK TIP!
Give every Explorer or Scout an index card with the names of his group members to carry along to help keep track of Adventurers. You might also give each volunteer an index card listing the order of the Discovery Sites each group will visit. Consider using colored index cards that match the group's assigned color and slipping them into clear plastic sleeves secured to a lanyard that volunteers can wear around their necks.

including signs, decorations, backgrounds, and details.

🍃 **Don't go it alone**: You may want to involve your whole church in creating Wildwood Forest! Invite youth, Bible study groups, senior citizens, and others to help create the Discovery Sites and the overall theme.

🌰 **Detailed instructions**: Everything you need to know to set up each Discovery Site is explained more thoroughly in each site guide.

🌰 **Climb Higher**: The guides for each individual Discovery Site give you several options for creating a detailed and imaginative forest! Encourage your Discovery Site Leaders to read through the decorating ideas in their guides and use their imagination to create their sites.

Wildwood Forest Discovery Sites

Every Discovery Site is carefully thought out to make it the most effective in helping children discover our untamable God. Find complete information on running each Discovery Site in the individual guides. Simply give the appropriate guide to the Discovery Site Leader and he or she has all they need for success. A complete leader's guide is provided for each site except Trailhead and Misty Meadow. The following information outlines each site in Wildwood Forest and offers suggestions for set-up.

Trailhead

This is the spot where the children line up in their groups each day before heading to the Wildwood Forest large-group assembly area, Misty Meadow. Many churches find it convenient to invite the children to arrive 15 minutes early. This gives them a chance to greet friends, find where they belong, and get into the spirit of VBS. It gives newcomers time to get placed in a group without missing any of the fun.

Your Trailhead time will run much more smoothly if you have a registration table set up every day in a prominent place where parents can bring their children and find out which color group they are in. This table will be busiest on the first day, but visitors and forgetful children will need it on subsequent days.

Be sure to take attendance during this Trailhead time. Depending on your time and space here and in Misty Meadow, you might also choose to use this time to make announcements, lead the Pledge of Allegiance, take offerings, and recognize birthdays. If you don't have a portable audio system for making announcements at Trailhead, you may want to save these items for the actual opening assembly.

Explorers, Scouts, and any other leaders who are free can use this time to introduce themselves and get to know the children.

Get-to-Know-You Games!

Here are some quick name and get-to-know-you games that Explorers and Scouts can do with their groups while waiting for Wildwood Forest to begin, or that leaders can do in any spare time.

• Stuff a sock with rice and tie it closed. Have Adventurers stand in a wide circle and gently toss the sock back and forth across the circle. Have Adventurers say the name of the person they're tossing the sock to or who tossed it to them.

• While Adventurers are standing in a line, have the first child in line say his own name; then have the second child in line say, "This is my friend _____. I'm _____." The third child says, "These are my friends _____ and _____. I'm _____." The fourth child says the first three names and adds on hers, and so on down the line.

• Have Adventurers sit or stand in a circle. They take turns tossing a colorful squishy ball in random order. Each person who receives the ball tells a brief fact about himself or herself, such as school name, number of people in family, or type of pet they have.

• Play a quick game of "favorites." Gather Adventurers around and choose someone to tell what their favorite part of a forest is—the trees, the moss, the plants, the animals, the fallen logs, and so on. All the other children who like that part of the forest raise their hands as well. Then choose another child to tell a favorite part of the forest. Continue this game throughout the week when you have a few extra minutes, having Adventurers share their favorite foods, colors, games, TV shows, movies, and so on.

Setting up Trailhead

Your Wildwood Forest Trailhead can be any open area that can accommodate all the VBS Adventurers at once, and provide them space to get organized. Choose a spot where the children will be able to find their color-coded group with their Explorers and Scouts and where they can listen to the instructions from leaders.

You may choose to have the Trailhead in your church's main lobby, foyer, or fellowship hall. Or you could plan your entrance to be outside the church's main doors or in a roped-off area of the parking lot. (If you choose an outdoor spot, have a backup plan for inclement weather.)

Be sure to have a registration table set up, where children can go to check in each day, get nametags, and be assigned to groups.

ORGANIZE THE GROUPS

Use these effective group-organizing techniques to get your VBS off to a great start every day!

• Paint theater flats or panels from large appliance boxes with each group's tree and color. Place these at the Trailhead and have children line up in front of them.

• Be sure the Explorers and Scouts are wearing T-shirts in the colors of their assigned groups. You might also want to give them color-coordinated bandannas to wear.

• Have extra Explorers or Scouts (not assigned to a group) free to help wanderers get to their groups. You might place some at the parking lot and at the church doors to guide children to their spots. Be sure to always have someone on the lookout for latecomers.

• You may want to get poster board in the five group colors—or color them orange, yellow, green, silver, and red—and list on each poster board the names of the children in those color-coded groups. Hang the posters where arriving children can stop and look for their names. Add visitor names each day.

• As children get to their assigned groups, have Explorers and Scouts give out color-coded bandannas.

QUICK TIP!
To get to the first Discovery Site from Misty Meadow, one of your groups will be led by the Explorers and Scouts to Great Oak Theater for the Bible drama. The other four groups will go to four other Discovery Sites at the same time. If you are overseeing the logistics of the week, use the information on pages 24–28 of the *Wildwood Forest Director's Guide* to plan the order in which the groups will visit the Discovery Sites.

QUICK TIP!
Children will be using their student books, *called Elementary Field Guides,* every day at Great Oak Theater. Be sure that the Great Oak Theater Discovery Site Leader is prepared with sharpened pencils and crayons, and remind the Explorers and Scouts to have the field guides available and ready for use as soon as they arrive at the Discovery Site.

Misty Meadow

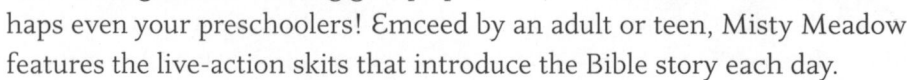

Opening Assembly

Misty Meadow is the location for your opening assemblies, where all the children are together in one big group—perhaps even your preschoolers! Emceed by an adult or teen, Misty Meadow features the live-action skits that introduce the Bible story each day.

To start off the day, Explorers and Scouts will lead their color-coded groups to Misty Meadow and direct them where to sit. The adult playing the role of Ranger Riley (the emcee) begins the session, welcoming the children and setting an upbeat tone. Be sure the actors are set up "backstage" before the children enter Misty Meadow. You'll find the skits beginning on page 32.

During the Misty Meadow opening assembly, the children will be introduced to the day's Bible story through the skit and will sing the Wildwood Forest VBS theme song, "Wild and Wonderful God," or other praise songs included in the *Wildwood Forest Praise Songs* CD. The music can be led with the Wildwood Forest CD, the sheet music found on the *Wildwood Forest Program Resources* CD-ROM (with someone playing piano or guitar), or with the music video (on the *Wildwood Forest Music and Promo* DVD) that has both the lyrics and the motions to the song.

Opening assembly is also the perfect time to present the Wildwood Forest VBS mission project, an excellent opportunity to let Adventurers make a difference in other children's lives. **Standing Tall Together** is explained with all other opening assembly options on pages 26–27.

The emcee of your opening assemblies should send out shimmering branches of enthusiasm. He or she should begin each day at Wildwood Forest with a grand welcome along these lines: **Welcome to Wildwood Forest VBS! The adventure begins in just a few minutes. Are you ready? Great! Everyone is invited along, so I hope you and you and you** (point to individual children) **are ready for the most incredible forest adventure you've ever been on. Let the adventure begin!** (Lead clapping and cheering.)

Setting up Misty Meadow

You will need a space big enough to seat all the Adventurers (on the floor or in chairs) with an up-front area where everyone can see Ranger Riley and the skit actors. You will probably need microphones (and therefore a sound system) for all four of them. Consider using your church's fellowship hall or sanctuary for Misty Meadow.

Edgy Extras!

You can give your assembly area the feel of a real forest. Use clip art from the *Wildwood Forest Promotional Materials* CD-ROM to create posters and signs featuring sites from Wildwood Forest. Use an overhead projector to shine pieces of the clip art on a wall or large piece of butcher paper, and trace them with a paintbrush or large marker. Use brown butcher paper or grocery bags to create large tree trunks around the room, sketching in bark lines with black marker. You can apply the tree trunks flat on the wall, or stuff newspaper under the trunks for a three-dimensional look. Ask church and staff members to lend you fake evergreen trees (be sure to label them with the lender's name) that you can set up on the outskirts of your meadow. Rent or buy a fog machine to create a truly misty atmosphere.

Great Oak Theater

Bible Drama

The leaders at Great Oak Theater will use the *Great Oak Theater Drama Guide* to lead Adventurers through an engaging and interactive Bible story. The teaching technique is drama with lots of variety! Every day the children will encounter the wild heart of God and discover that's right where they belong.

The daily Bible drama is simple to present. But your Great Oak Theater leaders can make it as elaborate as they want. Each lesson includes creative **Climb Higher** ideas to enhance the Bible drama. **Climb Higher** often includes ideas for additional supplies or for making the drama more realistic. Each day also includes a Contemplating the Adventure option which will allow Adventurers to quiet their hearts and reflect on the day's Bible story and **Live It!**

The Great Oak Theater leaders will present the same Bible drama five times in one day—once to each of the five groups that rotate to this Discovery Site. The same Bible story presentation will work for all the elementary (K–5) age levels. Please note: Salvation lessons for this year's VBS are found in Great Oak Theater on Days 3 and 5.

All the Bible dramas, plans, and options for the Great Oak Theater Discovery Site are in the *Great Oak Theater Drama Guide*.

Setting up Great Oak Theater

Choose a spot for Great Oak Theater where there is room for dramas based on the Bible stories. Adventurers will often be taking part in the dramas, and you'll need a wide-open room or space. You don't need a stage—just a clear spot where everyone can see and interact. A large classroom with tables and chairs removed works well. You won't need a sound system for these dramas unless you hold Great Oak Theater in an exceptionally large room.

QUICK TIP!
Though only the Great Oak Theater leaders present the entire Bible story, be sure all your leaders know the Wildwood Forest Bible stories and **Live It!** to tie into their Discovery Sites. Summaries of each day's Bible story are found in the front of each individual guide.

VineLand Adventure Course

Games

When groups journey to VineLand Adventure Course, they'll dive into challenging Bible application activities and games. All the games outlined in the *VineLand Adventure Course Games Guide* are full of super Bible twists and turns. These activities get the children interacting both with each other and with the daily Bible story content.

Every lesson offers two fun, forest-themed games or activities. We suggest that the game leader consider setting up both games and having them ready for the Adventurers. When children finish with one, the next game is ready to play. The VineLand Adventure Course leader will present the same game or activity five times in one day—once to each of the five groups that rotate to this Discovery Site.

Setting up VineLand Adventure Course

VineLand Adventure Course will need wide-open space, clear of furniture. You might even consider holding this Discovery Site outdoors—just make sure you have a backup plan in case of bad weather. If you're indoors, remove tables and chairs from the room or push them securely to the side. The only equipment or supplies you'll need here are the ones listed in the games and activities in the *VineLand Adventure Course Games Guide*. You can also find all the VineLand Adventure Course game instructions, along with prep time, in the guide.

Treetop Art Studio

Crafts

When Adventurers visit Treetop Art Studio, they'll create projects to take home as reminders of the life application points they learned at Wildwood Forest VBS.

The leader of the Discovery Site will choose between two creative crafts each day. The choice will depend on availability of supplies, level of difficulty, and the particular application. Throughout the week, the craft choices will cover the day's **Live It!** along with the Bible story content and the Wildwood Forest theme.

Once a craft is chosen, the Treetop Art Studio leader will teach the same craft all day, to all five groups of Adventurers. The next day the leader chooses another craft to teach to all five groups, and so on.

All the craft ideas to be used in the Treetop Art Studio, along with step-by-step instructions, photos, and options, are in the *Treetop Art Studio Craft Guide*.

Setting up Treetop Art Studio

Provide tables for craft time. To allow for more flexibility and elbow room, try removing chairs from the space. Most Adventurers will not mind standing while they work. Plan to store your craft supplies in this area, or keep all the supplies in a box or tote to bring to this Discovery Site every day.

Harvest Grove
Large-Group Snack Time

In the middle of your VBS time, everyone will be ready for refreshments and a break. Plan to have all the Adventurers come together in a place that's safe to have food and drinks. The Discovery Site Leaders (and optional helpers) for this part of Wildwood Forest will prepare the snacks ahead of time, choosing from two yummy, simple snacks that reinforce Bible learning! All the recipes and instructions for each day's snack options can be found in the *Harvest Grove Snack Guide*.

Explorers and Scouts will lead their groups to the eating area and help them get seated. You may choose to seat Adventurers around tables, or have them sit on the floor. You might even find it convenient to have them picnic outside on the grass or on beach towels.

You could choose to have Adventurers pick up their snacks by walking through a line, buffet-style, or you could have helpers bring the refreshments to the children once they're seated. Before everyone gets their refreshments, be sure to have a leader, pastor, or yourself lead a prayer to ask God to bless the good food he provides—and to ask him to bless the Adventurers as well.

Encourage children to sit back and relax during this time as they enjoy chatting with friends. After snack is a great time for free play outside if the weather is nice. There's lots of energetic activity to come!

Setting up Harvest Grove

Your church may already have a location where food can be served and which can accommodate all the children. If so, you may want to use this spot for Harvest Grove. Another option is to take the children outdoors or use another large room indoors. If you can't hold all the children in one spot, you can keep them in their groups and serve their refreshments at the end of their third Discovery Site, bringing the snacks to those Discovery Site areas.

Bring It to Life!

If using one central, indoor area, you can decorate this room using clip art pictures (see *Wildwood Forest Promotional Materials* CD-ROM). You may even want to recycle props from other areas (such as Trailhead). Inside the Wildwood Forest Decorating Pack you can find stencils and paper vines to further decorate your walls. You'll find more ideas for decorating this Discovery Site in the *Harvest Grove Snack Guide*.

QUICK TIP!
Print each day's Key Verse and **Live It!** on separate 8 ½ x 11-inch papers and post them in the room for children to see. Reinforce both elements by reviewing the Key Verse as soon as children enter the Treetop Art Studio and then having children shout the "password" for the day (the day's **Live It!**) as they exit the Discovery Site.

The Heights

Bible Memory and Music

Adventurers visiting The Heights are in for a treat—awesome praise music videos to get them on their feet, singing and doing actions. Each video has the words and music that will reinforce the day's Bible focus. Play one video every day. You may choose to review videos as the week continues.

The Starter Kit comes with a *Wildwood Forest Music and Promo* DVD to use with a TV/DVD player or a projection screen and sound system. The leader simply has to press the button and enthusiastically lead the singing as he or she stands next to the screen. The music videos will teach Adventurers the songs and actions.

For those churches without access to a TV with a DVD player, the sheet music for all ten Wildwood Forest songs can be found on the *Wildwood Forest Program Resources* CD-ROM. You can have someone play the piano, lead with guitar, or simply sing a cappella. Feel free to run this Discovery Site with or without technology!

The Heights also provides the option for children to memorize the day's Key Verse. The leader can find a fun Bible memory activity or game for each lesson in The Heights guide as well. The leader at The Heights will use the same DVD songs and Bible memory activities with all five groups that rotate through each day.

Setting up The Heights

Choose a location for The Heights that can accommodate a TV with a DVD player or projection unit with a screen and sound, if you will be using the *Wildwood Forest Music and Promo* DVD for this Discovery Site. You might even be

Wildwood Forest Scavenger Search

As children roam Wildwood Forest, they will experience countless moments filled with fun, excitement, and the awe and wonder of God. And just when they think they've discovered everything the forest has to offer, they will stumble across another wild adventure: the Wildwood Forest Scavenger Search.

The Scavenger Search is a simple and fun spotlight on the week's lessons. Each day at The Heights, children will find clues to a special message. The message will read, "God's voice thunders in marvelous ways; he does great things beyond our understanding" (Job 37:5). Each day, The Heights Discovery Site Leader will hide clues on strips of paper somewhere in their area and place a small leaf near where each word is hidden. When Adventurers arrive at The Heights, they'll search for the clues. When all the papers have been found, the children will read the words aloud and write them in their student books, called the *Elementary Field Guide*. By the end of the week, the collected words will form a special message for your Adventurers. Your job (or the job of the emcee) will be to "decode" the message at the closing event of the final day.

able to double up using your Misty Meadow location for this rotation if that is the best spot for using a sound system, screen, and other audiovisual equipment.

Be sure every Adventurer will be able to see the music videos, and allow enough space for them to move freely.

Glow Rock Hideaway

Laboratory

The unique and exciting Glow Rock Hideaway Discovery Site is sure to be the highlight of VBS for many of your Adventurers. Adventurers will get to see and touch God's amazing power through simple, yet astounding, science experiments that highlight God's wild heart. Each day's experiment draws children into a deeper understanding of the **Live It!** and Bible lesson.

The Glow Rock Hideaway Discovery Site Leader will find simple instructions for leading each day's experiment in the *Glow Rock Hideaway Lab Guide*. There is also a colorful, creative student lab sheet for each day's experiment located in the Wildwood Forest elementary student books, called *Elementary Field Guides*.

Setting up Glow Rock Hideaway

At Glow Rock Hideaway, Adventurers will watch and participate in exciting science experiments. Set up a demonstration table at the front where supplies can be displayed and the leader can conduct the experiment itself. Arrange any children's tables nearby. If possible, have children sit or stand at their own tables, because they will do parts of the experiment and need a place that's conducive to doing experiments and writing in their field guides. Also make sure that every child can easily see the demonstration table.

Back to Misty Meadow

Large Group Wrap-Up

Return to Misty Meadow to briefly wrap up Wildwood Forest VBS for the day. All the groups gather back together for announcements, distribution of take-homes, and dismissal. You might even include a "teaser" or clues of what Adventurers will experience the next day. This is the chance to make sure that all sweaters, hats, crafts, and papers are accounted for—which will be easy with the Explorers and Scouts carrying all these in a laundry basket! You can make this visit to Misty Meadow as short or as long as you need. Your Misty Meadow will also be a safe, central location for parents to pick up their children.

QUICK TIP!
Children will be using their field guides every day at The Heights. Be sure that The Heights Discovery Site Leader is prepared with sharpened pencils, and remind the Explorers and Scouts to have the field guides available and ready for use as soon as they arrive at the Discovery Site.

QUICK TIP!
If you'd like to project the words onto a screen for the children to follow along with, complete lyrics are found on the *Wildwood Forest Program Resources* CD-ROM.

 The *Wildwood Forest Music and Promo* DVD and *Wildwood Forest Praise Songs* CD include two praise songs and two hymns in addition to the five daily songs and theme song. These four additional songs further enhance children's adventure into the wild heart of God. Preview the songs before VBS begins and use them during The Heights and your opening and closing assemblies. You can purchase additional CDs, available at www.davidc-cook.com/vbs, to give to the children at the beginning of the week. This will give them even more time to get to know these fun songs.

Field Guide—Learning Tool and Souvenir!

The Wildwood Forest elementary student book, called the *Elementary Field Guide,* is a colorful learning tool you'll want to keep handy every day. Each student will need a field guide of his or her own to use at the daily Discovery Sites and to take home and share with their families.

Each day's lesson will correspond to four pages in the field guide. On the first page, you'll find a kid-size summary of the Bible story that is the foundation for the Discovery Site activities. Adventurers will use the second page when they visit Great Oak Theater. The activities in the field guide are experiential and interactive, to help children remember the Bible story and apply it to their own lives. On page three of each day in the field guide, Adventurers will find instructions for the Glow Rock Hideaway experiment. They'll be revved up and ready to go when they realize they can duplicate the science activity at home! They'll also get a chance to complete a couple of fun activities related to the science experiment when they're at Glow Rock Hideaway. The final page contains activities Adventurers can do at home on their own or with their families.

At the end of the book is an empty page for autographs—a great way to remember VBS friends! Adventurers will also find a colorful map of Wildwood Forest on the back cover of their section—this is where they will record the clues from each day's Scavenger Search at The Heights.

Parents benefit from the field guide as well. The book includes an eight-page pull-out parent section. Remove this section from each book at the beginning of your VBS and send it home with children on the first day. That way parents will know what their children are learning at Wildwood Forest—the Bible story, Key Verse, and **Live It!** statement for each day's adventure. Inside the front cover, parents will find some tips on how to use the parent section as a discipleship tool that lets them help their children connect to the spiritual truths growing out of Wildwood Forest. The parent section includes activities the family can do together to reinforce the lessons children learn at Wildwood Forest.

Each field guide has holes punched in it so Adventurers can personalize the binding. Separate the parent pages from the books right away, then provide Adventurers with leather cord, twine, string, or different colors of yarn so they can tie the book together. You can do this at craft time, snack time, or during Trailhead, when Adventurers first receive their books.

When Wildwood Forest ends, Adventurers can take home the field guide as a souvenir of their adventure. As they look through the pages of the book, they'll remember the fabulous Bible story presentations, Key Verses, and **Live It!** truths. Make the most of the field guide! Children will learn with it and remember good times with it—and parents will appreciate how it helps them come alongside their children's developing faith.

Daily Opening Assemblies

Misty Meadow is the location for your opening assemblies when all the children are together in one big group—perhaps even your preschoolers! Emceed by an adult or teen, Misty Meadow's big feature is the live-action skit. There are four main sections to present to your Adventurers: Welcome Time, Mission Project Update, Skit, and Announcements. Following is a summary of each section to guide you in planning and conducting the opening assembly at Misty Meadow each day.

Welcome Time

To start off the day, Explorers and Scouts will lead their color-coded groups from Trailhead (the registration and sign-in area) to Misty Meadow and direct them where to sit. The emcee will welcome the children and set an upbeat tone. **Hello, Adventurers! Welcome to Wildwood Forest. This week we will study God's Word together to take ourselves on a daring adventure into the heart of God. So strap on your gear and get ready to hike into Wildwood Forest!**

Misty Meadow Opening Assembly Can Include:

- The Wildwood Forest theme song, "Wild and Wonderful God," and other praise songs that are included in the *Wildwood Forest Praise Songs* CD. Use the *Wildwood Forest Praise Songs* CD, the sheet music with someone playing piano or guitar (found on the *Wildwood Forest Program Resources* CD-ROM), or the music video (on the *Wildwood Forest Music and Promo* DVD, which includes song lyrics and motions.
- Wildwood Forest VBS **Standing Tall Together: Serving in Ukraine** mission project presentation and prayer time. (See pages 26 for details.)
- Additional elements led by the emcee, director, pastor, or other leader:
  - Opening prayer
  - Offering
  - Reminder for children to search for the day's Scavenger Search clue at The Heights (see page 26 for details).
  - Introduction of the Key Verse and the day's **Live It!**

Wildwood Forest Scavenger Search

During the opening assembly on Day 1, introduce children to the Scavenger Search by following this script. (See page 22 for more details.)

I have to tell you about another adventure we'll be taking this week. It's so much fun I just can't wait! It's a Scavenger Search! It's kind of like a treasure hunt and a word scramble all in one. Every day at The Heights, one of our Discovery Sites, you'll find hidden clues. Your teacher will tell you what to look for. The first Adventurers to find the clues get to read them aloud. Write the clue on the back page of your field guide. Hold up a sample field guide opened to a Scavenger Search page. At the very end of Wildwood Forest VBS, we'll figure out what the mysterious message is! Have fun and see if you can gather all the clues. Are you ready to do some detecting? Great! Give yourselves a big cheer. Lead the children in a loud cheer.

Mission Project

During each day's opening assembly, your emcee (yourself, your VBS director, or another volunteer) will collect the money and Prayer Trees for the Wildwood Forest mission project (see page 53 of the *Wildwood Forest Director's Guide* for more information), give an update about the project, and conduct a small-group prayer time for children in the Ukraine. Before VBS begins each day, hand out the day's prayer cards to each Explorer or Scout (see below for more information). They will distribute the cards to each child in their group before the opening assembly begins or before prayer time. Let Explorers and Scouts know that they need to seat their groups together to help prayer time move quickly and seamlessly. In addition, an at-home mission project element is available. In this portion, children complete a simple paper-based project (called Prayer Trees) for the Ukrainian children and families can contribute to the project together. More detailed information on this year's project begins on page 53 of the *Wildwood Forest Director's Guide*.

Mission Update

If you are participating in the mission project, you'll find scripts for each day's opening time in the *Wildwood Forest Director's Guide*. These scripts give children information about the project and real-life stories of children in Ukraine who have been touched by the love of Jesus and the help of others. Feel free to use the scripts word for word, or as a launching point for sharing your own thoughts and information.

Prayer Time

After the mission project update, ask the Adventurers to take out their prayer cards and hold them in their hands. Adventurers should already be sitting together with their groups, but have them quickly form prayer circles along with the group's Explorers and/or Scouts. Then have each group say a quick prayer for the children on their cards. Let

QUICK TIP!

If you find it difficult to fit small group prayer time into the opening assembly, ask Explorers to set aside a few minutes for prayer with the Ukraine prayer cards during Trailhead. You can also consider extending your opening assembly time by beginning a few minutes earlier.

everyone know that while they are welcome to pray out loud, they aren't required to. Ask leaders to join in the prayers and to encourage Adventurers who don't want to pray out loud to pray silently in their hearts.

When everyone is ready, give prayer prompts that will help Adventurers pray for specific details about the Ukrainian children on their cards (see below for ideas). Each group may have a few different cards, so encourage each Adventurer to pray for his or her own child. They can pray for:

- The child's family
- The child's education
- The child's hobbies
- The child's health
- The child's spiritual life
- The Bibles that are being sent to children like these
- Any other request for the Ukrainian child! Let Adventurers come up with their own.

After two or three minutes, close by saying something like: **Dear Jesus, you know each of the children on these cards. We pray that you would watch over them and help us to show them your amazing love. Thank you for the opportunity to pray for each of them. In Jesus' name, amen.**

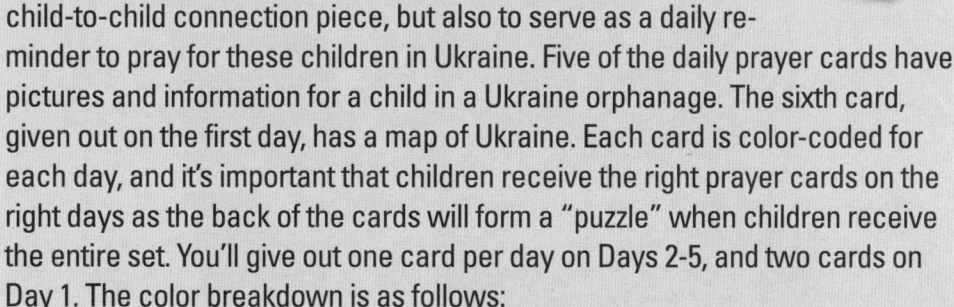

Prayer Cards

As a part of the Standing Tall mission project, you can purchase prayer cards for the Adventurers to learn more about children in Ukraine. These cards are designed to not only be a fun informational and child-to-child connection piece, but also to serve as a daily reminder to pray for these children in Ukraine. Five of the daily prayer cards have pictures and information for a child in a Ukraine orphanage. The sixth card, given out on the first day, has a map of Ukraine. Each card is color-coded for each day, and it's important that children receive the right prayer cards on the right days as the back of the cards will form a "puzzle" when children receive the entire set. You'll give out one card per day on Days 2-5, and two cards on Day 1. The color breakdown is as follows:

Day 1: Red and purple	Day 4: Orange
Day 2: Blue	Day 5: Yellow
Day 3: Green	

If you would like a longer, activity-based prayer time, consider adding a few minutes to your opening or closing assembly. Have fun praying for children in Ukraine by using the prayer cards in small prayer groups. When Adventurers form groups, have them pray for something specific about the children on their cards, such as the children's families or the country they live in. Have a few leaders oversee the activities and the prayer time. Ask the Adventurers to look at their prayer cards as you call out one of the following instructions:

- Find others in the room with the same prayer card as you.
- Find others who have children the same age as yours.
- Get into a group according to where your child lives.
- Everyone who has a boy should form one group. Those with girls form another.
- If you have similar interests or hobbies as the child on your card, form a group to the left. If your interests are different, form a group to the right.

You can also form prayer circles within the color groups (for example, all Orange Aspens will be in a group). Print a map of Ukraine and ask each Adventurer to locate their child's hometown, then have the group pray for those cities and the people in them.

Live-Action Skit

After you've given the update on the mission project, you're ready to introduce the day's Bible story and **Live It!** through a skit. Be sure the actors are set up "backstage" before Adventurers enter Misty Meadow. You'll find the daily skit scripts beginning on page 32.

Announcements

At the end of the opening assembly, take the time to make announcements. This is a great time to recognize any birthdays and welcome new friends. Before children begin their adventure in Wildwood Forest, give them a few parting words: **It's time to begin today's trek into Wildwood Forest! Your Explorers and Scouts can now take you to the first Discovery Site. Have fun today! I'll see you later.**

Daily Closing Assemblies

Head back to Misty Meadow to briefly wrap up Wildwood Forest VBS for the day. With all groups together, you can spend time on the following:

- Thank the children for coming, and give a "teaser" of what's happening the next day so children can look forward to it.
- Have Explorers and Scouts distribute the Adventurers' crafts from Treetop Art Studio. These will have been stored in the laundry basket or crate that the Explorers and Scouts carry with the group.
- Have Explorers and Scouts pass out any personal items the Adventurers brought—sweaters, hats, sunglasses. These also will be in the laundry baskets.
- Ask Explorers and Scouts to collect the children's bandannas and field guides to use again the next day.
- Remind children of any announcements and recognize any birthdays you may have missed earlier.
- Review the day's Wildwood Forest Scavenger Search clues, making sure that every child has the correct clues written down on the appropriate lines. You can ask Explorers and Scouts to circulate among the children, helping those who need a hand with writing clues that may have been missed.
- Remind children to bring money for **Standing Tall Together: Serving in Ukraine**, and make an announcement of how much money they raised that day. Show them the leaves that represent the day's donations.
- If you have time to fill, sing "Wild and Wonderful God" or one of the praise songs, or have groups repeat the day's Key Verse from memory.
- Have Adventurers wait in the assembly area, at Trailhead, or in another safe spot for parents to pick them up. The Explorers and Scouts should engage the children in games or conversation while waiting and stay with their groups until the last child has been picked up.

Wildwood Forest Day 5 Closing Program

As the finale of the Wildwood Forest VBS experience, the closing program is designed to celebrate the wild nature of our incredible God. It's a great opportunity for your church to reach out to families who sent their children to VBS but do not attend church regularly. The final skit offers relevant principles that children and parents can easily recognize and apply to their lives. And the participation by the children is just plain fun! Make sure Adventurers invite their families, friends, and neighbors to share in this celebration. The traditional program is designed to follow this basic schedule:

15 minutes	Welcome: welcome by Lead Explorer, prayer by pastor
30 minutes	Program: skit, songs, sharing
15 minutes	Presentations: missions, awards
30 minutes	Refreshments: leaders mingle to meet visitors and children's families

Fifteen minutes before the closing program begins, play music from the *Wildwood Forest Praise Songs* CD or some other Christian children's music softly through the sound system.

Welcome

When it's time to begin, play the VBS theme song, "Wild and Wonderful God," while children enter from the back of the sanctuary or auditorium. Adventurers can step in time with the music and line up in front of the church, facing the audience. If a particularly ambitious group of young performers happens to be among your attendees, they might choose to choreograph the processional to this song during the week and perform it while other children are entering, lining up, and singing. After the theme song, the director welcomes the audience; then the pastor offers an opening prayer.

Program

The pastor or Lead Explorer introduces the closing skit (found on page 47). You'll need the same actors/actresses who performed in the opening assembly skits, as well as the same props.

After the skit, let Adventurers come up and share highlights of Wildwood Forest VBS. Arrange this sharing during the week to give children time to prepare. Sharing can happen in many forms. A group of children could briefly demonstrate each Discovery Site from Wildwood Forest. For example, ask Adventurers to bring up a craft and explain to the audience what it helps them remember. Or, have a couple of Adventurers demonstrate a simple game or recite a couple Key Verses. You might interview several children about things they liked about VBS or what they learned. Be sure to ask specific questions that Adventurers can answer easily.

During this time you might also have Adventurers perform some of the praise songs from the *Wildwood Forest Praise Songs* CD. You can project the lyrics onto a screen or even play the music videos as the children sing along. Select songs ahead of time to work on during the week so you can be sure everyone knows them well. Be sure to encourage the rest of the audience to participate!

Presentations

Take a few minutes to present this year's VBS mission project, **Standing Tall Together.** (See details on pages 53-57 of the *Wildwood Forest Director's Guide* and page 26 of this guide.) Be sure to share how children contributed to the mission project throughout Wildwood Forest VBS.

Thank the volunteers who contributed their time to VBS. Recognize the Adventurers as well. The Lead Explorer might give each child who attended a Certificate of Completion (on the *Wildwood Forest Program Resources* CD-ROM or from the *Wildwood Forest Director's Guide*). Thank the Adventurers and their families for participating.

Close with a prayer, followed by a reprise of the children singing this year's VBS theme song.

Refreshments

Provide light refreshments to encourage families and visitors to stay and chat. Ahead of time, encourage leaders to use this opportunity to meet Adventurers' families and friends. This is a great way to reach out to people who seldom visit a church.

Along with Certificates of Completion (personalize the certificate found in the *Wildwood Forest Director's Guide* and on the *Wildwood Forest Program Resources* CD-ROM), you may choose to give Adventurers a gift that will be a reminder of what they learned at Wildwood Forest. You can order Wildwood Forest photo frames and Bible Memory Backpack Danglers at www.davidccook.com/vbs. They make great keepsakes!

Intergenerational Closing Option

This option allows for a fun two-hour family experience. Follow this schedule:

10 minutes	**Welcome and organizing**—As families arrive, greet them and place them into five groups. If any children do not have family present, team them up with a friend's family. Assign an Explorer or Scout to each group.
75 minutes	**Visiting Wildwood Forest**—Have each group start at a different Discovery Site. Groups then rotate through each of the five Discovery Sites, spending 15 minutes at each one. The regular leaders and helpers should run the Discovery Sites, allowing families to do one of the site's activities that the Adventurers experienced during the week. Keep track of time and give a signal for the groups to move on to the next Discovery Site. Be sure to allow for travel time between stops.
20 minutes	**Closing assembly**—Gather for a closing awards assembly and refreshments. Invite the whole group to sing the VBS theme song as you play the DVD and project it onto a screen. Then enjoy refreshments together. See additional ideas in the Closing Program section.

Opening Assembly Skits

Bible Story
Gideon's Fight
(Judges 7:1–8, 16–22)

Key Verse
It is not by sword or spear that the LORD saves; for the battle is the LORD'S. (1 Samuel 17:47)

Live It!
God is undefeatable.

QUICK TIP!
If needed, the role of Ranger McPhearless in each of these skits can easily be played by the emcee, Ranger Riley. Simply use Ranger Riley's name in place of "Ranger McPhearless" and tweak the opening lines of each day's skit as needed.

Script Day 1

Description of Set

Use greenery to create a backdrop for the stage area: a combination of real potted plants and trees along with fake trees (including fake Christmas trees) and plants will work great. A three-panel cardboard backdrop with trees drawn on it can be added behind these plants if needed. Place a few additional potted plants around the stage area and scatter leaves (from silk plants or cut from construction paper) along the ground. Include two upside-down buckets (painted brown or covered in construction paper) to look like tree stumps; the characters will use these stumps as seats during some of the skits.

Cast:

- **Ranger McPhearless:** He/she serves in the role of a lead Scout and should be dressed like one (Wildwood Forest T-shirt, bandanna, etc.). McPhearless is an expert on both God and nature, with an adventurous spirit. McPhearless will tell Adventurers (and other characters) more about the adventures they can expect that day in the Wildwood Forest. McPhearless should be fearless, fun, and kind. Just about everything he/she does is big and overdramatic. A burst of adventure theme music plays each time McPhearless enters the stage.

- **Quint:** Quint is a nerdy, urbanite teen who is totally out of place in the Wildwood Forest. He should be dressed in outdoor gear, such as boots, camouflage clothing, a fishing vest, and an outdoor hat. He should also be lugging around lots of outdoor equipment, such as a mountain-climbers' backpack, binoculars (around his neck), a safety whistle (around his neck), a compass (around his neck), snowshoes strapped to his pack, and sunscreen, maps, and bug spray stuffed in his pockets. The actor playing Quint should ham things up, making Quint the ultimate (lovable) nerd with an exaggerated nasal voice and lots of goofy expressions.

- **Mimi:** Mimi, Quint's teenage cousin, is a complete city slicker. She should be dressed in clothing not appropriate for the outdoors, such as high heels and a modest dress with a fishing vest on top and a backpack strapped on. Mimi should have an elaborate hair-do and bright red lipstick. She is also carrying a lot of excess equipment, though some of it should be obviously inappropriate for outdoor adventures, such as a curling iron, hair dryer, hand mirror, set of curlers, hair gels, an iron, etc. Mimi is a loving cousin who, like Quint, is completely out of touch with what an adventure in Wildwood Forest actually entails.

RANGER RILEY: Well, Adventurers, let me introduce you to the lead Scout of Wildwood Forest, Ranger McPhearless!

(Ranger McPhearless enters dramatically as his/her theme music plays, and high-fives Ranger Riley. Ranger Riley returns the high-five and exits. Quint and Mimi are behind the audience, but not backstage.)

RANGER MCPHEARLESS: Hey, Adventurers! I'll bet you're here to have a great adventure. Well, I love adventures too! Hey, whenever I call out, "adventure calls!" I want you to say, "woo-hoo!" Got it? Okay, let's try it a few times. Adventure calls! *(Waits for Adventurers to respond, "woo-hoo!")* I can't hear you. Adventure calls! *("Woo-hoo!")* That's better. Let's try it one more time. Adventure calls!

QUINT: *(In a nasal voice from the back of the room after campers yell, "Woo-hoo!")* I'm not sure that there's a cause for celebration, Scout McPhearless, I mean Mr. Ranger, sir. Is this adventure entirely safe and allergy free? *(Sneezes loudly)*

RANGER MCPHEARLESS: *(Surprised, looking around)* Who said that?

QUINT: *(Sniffing loudly)* I did, Mr. Scout McPhearless Ranger, sir. My name's Quint. *(Quint and Mimi walk toward the stage area. Mimi is talking on her cell phone. They are lugging a great deal of camping and outdoor equipment.)*

MIMI: *(Into her cell phone)* No, I can't go to the mall today.

QUINT: I'm assuming that whole "wild" part of Wildwood Forest is just advertising. There's nothing actually wild here, is there … nothing dangerous?

MIMI: He said what? Tell him that she said that I said that you said that he didn't say what you said you thought she heard.

RANGER MCPHEARLESS: *(With much bravado)* As the lead scout, I'll keep you safe in Wildwood Forest as you learn about God and how He made no leaf too small, or tree too big.

QUINT: Oh my! I hope I'm up on my shots. And my allergies won't be too happy about this …ah … ah … ah-CHOO!

MIMI: No. Mom said that if I go here with Quint, I can totally dye my hair any color I want. Hello? Are you there? *(She presses buttons. Her cell phone has lost its signal.)*

RANGER MCPHEARLESS: *(Clears throat and looks at Mimi a little strangely)* Okay, well, the Adventurers and I are going to be learning about God's wild nature and Bible history. Are you with us?

QUINT: I don't know. Will this trek into Wildwood Forest be troublous … or treasonous … or noxious … or nauseous?

MIMI: My phone's lost its connection. I have an emergency. *(Asking audience members)* Quick, hand me your cell phone. I need to text someone.

RANGER MCPHEARLESS: *(Taps Mimi on the shoulder)* Um, sorry to say, but no cell phone will get reception here.

MIMI: What kind of place is this?

QUINT: *(Sniffing)* I want a guarantee in writing that there will be no risks, dangers, surprises, or icky food.

MIMI: If we can get to a mall with a food court, we'll be OK. Where's your nearest mall, scout-man?

RANGER MCPHEARLESS: We don't have a mall here …

QUINT AND MIMI: What?

RANGER MCPHEARLESS: You signed up for an adventure at Wildwood Forest. It's going to be a week of surprises, risks, and new experiences! Adventure calls! *("Woo-hoo!")*

QUINT AND MIMI: *(Hugging each other as if they're facing a fate worse than death)* Noooo! *(Their camping gear gets in the way and they lose their balance and fall to the ground.)*

RANGER MCPHEARLESS: *(Gesturing excitedly, not noticing that the cousins have fallen)* As we explore the forest, we're going to get to know our awesome, amazing, wondrous God!

MIMI: No manicures? No massages? It's a real forest?

QUINT: A wild forest filled with surprises?

MIMI: *(Getting to her feet)* I'm not sure I'm up to this.

QUINT: *(Stands and takes stock of what he's brought with him)* I don't have the right equipment for scary, dangerous stuff.

RANGER MCPHEARLESS: It looks like you brought the whole camping store.

MIMI: Tell me I'll be able to plug in my blow dryer and curling iron.

(Ranger McPhearless shakes his/her head no.)

QUINT: Mimi, I've never seen you without four hours of hair and makeup. It may be worth staying just to see how you'll look at the end of a week.

(As Mimi says her next line, Quint watches an imaginary mosquito.)

MIMI: Don't be mean, Quint. You wouldn't last a whole day without your Internet connection and video games. I could last longer on this little adventure thing-ey than you could.

QUINT: *(Slaps the mosquito as it lands on his arm)* Did you see that, Mimi? A

real, live mosquito. And I killed it! I didn't know I had it in me ...
(Sneezes)

MIMI: That was amazing. There wasn't even a bug zapper nearby.

QUINT: *(Amazed)* That was a wild creature from the forest.

MIMI: I wish I had my camera. It would have so been on my Facebook site.

QUINT: *(Proud)* What a battle ... what a fight! I've already started the adventure! Bring it on!

MIMI: Wait till I tell Mary to tell Ina's best friend's sister. You'll be famous!

RANGER MCPHEARLESS: Er, slapping a mosquito officially doesn't count as a "battle," Quint, but today we're going to learn about a real battle. A man named Gideon was the commander of the Israelite army, and they fought a real enemy.

QUINT: I think I've heard of the Israelites. Aren't they God's chosen people in the Bible?

RANGER MCPHEARLESS: Right. They were facing a horrible, terrible, powerful, enemy army from Midian. It was gigantic.

QUINT: Were the Israelites scared?

RANGER MCPHEARLESS: Many were, but God was with them, and he cannot be defeated. He is undefeatable.

QUINT: I get scared a lot. I'd like to hear about Gideon.

MIMI: If you're going to listen, I will too.

RANGER MCPHEARLESS: That's great. Come with me, and we'll get started. Adventure calls! *("Woo-hoo!")*

(Ranger McPhearless bounds dramatically offstage. Quint and Mimi straggle behind, lugging all their gear with them. Quint sneezes loudly as they exit.)

Script Day 2

Cast:
• Ranger McPhearless, Quint, and Mimi

Props:
• Quint and Mimi's outdoor gear; tree stumps and limbs, set up as a small obstacle course; and Ranger McPhearless's adventure theme music.

RANGER RILEY: Before we go any further, Adventurers, let's take a look at what our friends Quint and Mimi are up to ...

Bible Story
The Fiery Furnace
(Daniel 3:1–29)

Key Verse
How awesome is the LORD Most High, the great King over all the earth!
(Psalm 47:2)

Live It!
God is unmatchable.

(Ranger Riley exits. Quint and Mimi walk onstage still carrying their packs and camping equipment. Quint is covered with dirt and twigs.)

MIMI: Don't worry, Quint. I'll make the mud pit a little shorter, and you won't fall in it and get all messy next time. Now here's your gold level.

(Mimi sits on a tree stump, and Quint begins the obstacle course—jumping over stumps and ducking under tree limbs.)

MIMI: Jump. Now jump again. Careful. Duck!

(Quint hams up being barely able to accomplish the first few jumps and sneezes at regular intervals. He doesn't duck under a branch in time and falls to the ground.)

MIMI: Do you want to do this or not? You just lost one of your lives, and now you have to start over.
QUINT: Why am I doing this, again?
MIMI: *(Mock-patiently holds up a portable game system)* Because the batteries in your portable game system died. You're playing a non-virtual video game, and I am being entertained. The batteries in my portable TV died too.

(Ranger McPhearless's adventure theme music plays.)

QUINT: What was that?
MIMI: Maybe you beat the level?

(Ranger McPhearless enters. He/she easily plays the obstacle course that Mimi has built without realizing it was supposed to be hard. Quint and Mimi watch in amazement.)

MCPHEARLESS: *(Energetically)* Good morning, Quint and Mimi. Are you ready for today's adventure? Adventure calls! *("Woo-hoo!")*
MIMI: I'm not an adventurous person, and I'm not used to living like this. Look at my hair—it's a mess.
QUINT: Your hair is the least of our concerns. I don't know if my allergies can handle all the wild creatures and huge trees. *(Sniffles and wipes his nose on his arm)*
MIMI: I keep thinking about our comfortable homes back in the city.
QUINT: Nothing compares to playing a video game or going on the Internet whenever I want.
MIMI: I broke a nail, and I had to put a blanket over my eyes last night to

block out the light from the stars. Even then, it took forever to fall asleep because I usually drift off while listening to music on my mp3 player.

QUINT: At home, I have walls and windows to keep out mosquitoes …

MIMI: My walk-in closet is full of high-heeled shoes …

QUINT: I have a jumbo-sized box of tissues …

MIMI: And I can use a mirror to put on my lipstick.

RANGER MCPHEARLESS: *(Patiently)* Instead of only looking at what you can't do, maybe you should think about what you can do.

MIMI: Like what?

RANGER MCPHEARLESS: I love being in Wildwood Forest. Sometimes, I find a place where I can be alone so I can listen to the sounds of the forest.

QUINT: A few more beeps and blips would be to my liking.

RANGER MCPHEARLESS: Sometimes at night, I lie on my back and watch the stars. There's nothing like star gazing and talking to God.

MIMI: The only stars I want to see are inside my favorite magazine.

RANGER MCPHEARLESS: *(Puts his/her arms around Quint and Mimi)* I know this isn't the vacation you had in mind, but it can still be awesome, if you let it. Adventure calls! *("Woo-hoo!")*

QUINT: To be honest, Ranger McPhearless, we don't fit in here. *(Sneezes)*

MIMI: And this whole experience isn't like anything we're used to.

RANGER MCPHEARLESS: Maybe today's lesson will help you. We're going to learn about three friends who didn't fit in either.

QUINT: Were they in a forest?

RANGER MCPHEARLESS: No, worse. They'd been captured during a war and taken to live in a foreign land.

QUINT: I'll bet the food was different.

MIMI: And the language.

RANGER MCPHEARLESS: But worst of all, the people in the new land, Babylon, worshipped false gods, and Shadrach, Meshach, and Abednego served the one true God.

MIMI: Why was that a problem? Quint and I go to different churches.

RANGER MCPHEARLESS: But you worship the same God. You merely go to different places to do it. Do you know how you feel like nothing here compares to your life in the city?

QUINT AND MIMI: Yes.

RANGER MCPHEARLESS: Shadrach, Meshach, and Abednego knew that nothing in the world compared to their God.

QUINT: He sounds unmatchable.

RANGER MCPHEARLESS: He is. But the king in that foreign land made a huge idol and demanded that everyone worship it. If anyone didn't, they'd be killed.

QUINT: Now that's dangerous.

RANGER MCPHEARLESS: Bowing down to an idol would have been a really big deal for them. The idol didn't compare to the true God—God is unmatchable.

MIMI: So what did they do?

QUINT: Yeah, what happened next?

RANGER MCPHEARLESS: Before I answer that, you have a choice to make. *(Starts to walk offstage, playfully gesturing for Quint and Mimi to follow)* You can keep playing your pretend video game or join the other Adventurers and find out what happened to Shadrach, Meshach, and Abednego. Adventure calls! *("woo-hoo!")*

(Ranger McPhearless winks at Quint and Mimi, then exits.)

QUINT: Maybe we should become an Adventurer … just for today.

MIMI: Okay. Who knows? We might even pick up some pointers on how to fit in better.

QUINT: Ah-choo! That would take a God who does miracles.

(Quint and Mimi follow Ranger McPhearless offstage, their equipment slowing them down.)

Script Day 3

RANGER RILEY: Okay, Adventurers, let's turn it over to Ranger McPhearless, who's going to tell us about the great things we've got planned for you today!

(Ranger McPhearless enters to Ranger McPhearless's adventure theme music. Quint and Mimi stand behind the audience. Mimi's hair does not look as if it has been combed.)

Bible Story
Paul and Silas's Night in Prison (Acts 16:16–34)

Key Verse
"Believe in the Lord Jesus, and you will be saved." (Acts 16:31)

Live It!
God is uncontainable.

RANGER MCPHEARLESS: Hello there, Adventurers. Are you ready to have some fun today? *(Waits for response)* **Adventure calls!** *("Woo-hoo!")*

MIMI: *(After the kids say, "Yeah!")* **Yeah! I'm ready!**

(Mimi hurries toward the stage, wobbling a bit on her high heels. She stops halfway and calls behind her.)

MIMI: Come on, Quint. Let's have some fun.

QUINT: *(Follows as he grumbles)* What has gotten into you, Miss I-No-Longer-Need-A-Hairbrush? You were as miserable as I was when we went to sleep last night.

MIMI: Stop complaining, Quint, and hurry up.

(Mimi has only a sensible backpack, but Quint lugs all of his outdoor gear and some of Mimi's onstage with him.)

MIMI: Hi, Ranger McPhearless.

RANGER MCPHEARLESS: *(Shocked)* Well, hello, Mimi. It's great to see you so … so … so … are you actually smiling?

MIMI: I can't wait to join in the fun with the other Adventurers today.

QUINT: *(To audience)* Mimi's hair is a mess, and she's still happy. *(Sniffs)* I don't get it.

(Quint sneezes and pulls out a large handkerchief to blow his nose loudly.)

RANGER MCPHEARLESS: That's great to hear, Mimi.

QUINT: What happened to you? Last night, you didn't like being in Wild-wood Forest.

MIMI: I've started to make friends with some of the other Adventurers. They're really nice.

RANGER MCPHEARLESS: Our Adventurers are pretty amazing! *(Gives thumbs up to Adventurers)* **Adventure calls!** *("Woo-hoo!")*

MIMI: And last night, I was trying to fall asleep with the blanket over my eyes, when I remembered what you said about lying on your back and watching the stars.

QUINT: Is that when you yelled, "Would somebody please turn off those awful stars?"

MIMI: No, that was earlier.

QUINT: How about when you yelled, "This blanket smells like Quint's armpits!"

MIMI: No, that was earlier too. When I pulled the blanket off my eyes, I looked at the stars. They were … amazing. I wondered why I'd never seen them like that before.

QUINT: It's a wild guess, but maybe it's because you were usually asleep when they came out. That means your eyes were shut. *(Sneezes)*

MIMI: Anyway, I started to think about God and what we've discovered about him so far this week. The stars made me think about how powerful and awesome God is.

QUINT: Mimi, you're not quite yourself this morning … I haven't heard you complain at all. Wait a minute. Are you sick? Do you have a twin? *(Sneezes)* Who are you and what have you done with my cousin?

MIMI: No, Quint, I don't feel sick, and I don't have a twin. I feel great.

RANGER MCPHEARLESS: Quint, your cousin is discovering how awesome and amazing God is. Isn't that great, Adventurers? *(Allow time for kids to respond.)*

MIMI: It is great. When I thought about how powerful God is, I started getting excited. *(Ham up the following line by punching the air, shouting in high and low voices, etc.)* I just wanted to shout, "Woo-hoo! Woo-hoo! Yeah! Yay! Bam!"

RANGER MCPHEARLESS: I think you're trying to say that you wanted to worship God.

MIMI: Yes, that's it. I wanted to worship God.

RANGER MCPHEARLESS: Mimi, you're going to enjoy our story today because it's about how Paul and Silas wanted God to know how great he is. Paul and Silas were two men from the Bible who told others about Jesus' love.

QUINT: Mimi may enjoy that story, but I won't. I'm in a horrible, outdoor place, and I don't see any reason to get excited about what God is doing for me. *(Dabs his nose with the handkerchief)*

RANGER MCPHEARLESS: Paul and Silas were in a much worse place.

QUINT: I doubt it. What could be worse than this?

RANGER MCPHEARLESS: *(Leaning forward and stage whispering)* A prison.

MIMI: *(Leans forward as well, matching McPhearless's stage whisper.)* Paul and Silas were in prison?

RANGER MCPHEARLESS: *(Still whispering)* Yeah.

QUINT: *(Loudly)* Okay, maybe that is a little worse. But they must have deserved it.

RANGER MCPHEARLESS: Actually, they didn't. They were put there because some people wanted to stop their message about God. But Paul and Silas worshipped God even in prison … and they found that God and his message of love were uncontainable.

MIMI: Just like I couldn't stop the stars from shining at night, God's plans weren't stopped because Paul and Silas were chained up in jail.

QUINT: I don't see the big deal. So they sang a few songs. I sang a few songs yesterday. *(Singing as if it were a dirge)* On top of spaghetti, all covered with cheese …

(Mimi puts her hand over Quint's mouth to stop him.)

RANGER MCPHEARLESS: Worship is more than singing a song, but songs are one way to tell God how excited you are about him. When Paul and Silas sang, something unexpected and amazing happened.

MIMI: What? What happened?

RANGER MCPHEARLESS: Follow me, and you'll find out! Adventure calls!

("Woo-hoo!")

(Ranger McPhearless exits dramatically.)

MIMI: I'm right behind you.

(Mimi helps Quint carry his gear.)

QUINT: Mimi, did you really mean all that stuff you said? What about all the danger? The risk? The ... *(Sneezes)* the wildness?

MIMI: We're here for the week. We may as well have some fun.

QUINT: I don't know, Mimi. *(Sneezes)* You may no longer care about combing your hair, but I'm still miserable.

MIMI: Just try to have a little fun today, okay?

QUINT: I'll try. *(Weakly)* Woo-hoo.

(Mimi and Quint exit. Quint gives a loud sneeze once he's offstage.)

Script Day 4

Cast:
• Ranger McPhearless, Quint, and Mimi. Mimi has some dirt smudged on her face and a few twigs and leaves sticking out of her messy hair. She is now wearing hiking boots instead of her high heel shoes.

Props:
• A pinecone placed on the top of something high onstage.

RANGER RILEY: Well, Adventurers, let's check back in with our friends Quint and Mimi.

(Ranger Riley exits stage. Mimi enters. Her hair is a worse mess than the day before.)

MIMI: *(Excited)* Hello, Adventurers! *(Waits for a response.)* Have you been learning a lot about God and his wonderful creation? *(Waits for a response.)* I've learned some things too. How many years do you think it

Bible Story
Elijah Meets God
in a Whisper
(1 Kings 19:9–18)

Key Verse
"Be still, and know that I am God." (Psalm 46:10)

Live It!
God is unpredictable.

takes a pineapple to grow to its full size? *(Waits for kids to guess. Gives them credit if they say the correct answer, or tells them that the answer is two if they don't.)* **Do you know how many different kinds of grass there are?** *(Waits for kids to guess. Gives them credit if they say the correct answer, or tells them that the answer is 9,500 if they don't.)* **What kind of tree is the largest in the world?** *(Waits for kids to guess. Gives them credit if they say the correct answer, or tells them that the answer is the giant sequoia if they don't.)* **Do you know where on its body a butterfly has its taste buds?** *(Waits for kids to guess. Gives them credit if they say the correct answer, or tells them that the answer is its feet if they don't.)*

(Mimi goes to look at a tree as Quint enters.)

QUINT: *(Hands cupped over mouth as he looks for her behind plants and trees, and even under one of the tree stumps)* Mimi … Mi-mi … Where are you, Mimi?

MIMI: Lookhere.

QUINT: What was that?

MIMI: Lookhere.

QUINT: What kind of bird is that?

MIMI: Quint, look over here.

QUINT: *(Shocked at her appearance)* What have you been doing?

MIMI: I've been exploring Wildwood Forest. I saw this really sparkly thing up a mountain. It turned out to be a rock reflecting the sun.

QUINT: Where is your lipstick? And your high-heel shoes?

MIMI: Back at the campsite. I couldn't climb trees in high-heel shoes. But enough about that. I'm glad you're here. Get down on all fours so I can stand on your back.

QUINT: What?

MIMI: There's a pinecone up there that I can't reach.

(During the following dialogue, Quint should lock his hands together to boost Mimi up to get the pinecone, but when that doesn't work, he should get on all fours and let her stand on his back to reach the pinecone.)

MIMI: It's so pretty.

QUINT: I don't understand you. You spend your days at the mall or texting on your cell phone and wearing high heels. What do you see in that pinecone?

MIMI: I want to see if I can get it.

QUINT: I never would have expected you to do anything like that.

MIMI: I've surprised myself too. I'm trying new things to see what I like to do. But I'm not the only one trying new things.

(Mimi climbs down from Quint's back, and Quint stands up.)

QUINT: I admit it. I put a marshmallow on an unsanitized stick yesterday ... and cooked it over a campfire. Then I ate it.

MIMI: That was adventurous of you.

QUINT: That was, wasn't it?

MIMI: And I've noticed that your allergies seem to be much better.

QUINT: Yeah ... it's strange, but I must be getting used to this forest or something. This has been an unusual ... and surprising ... and unpredictable week.

MIMI: For me too.

(Ranger McPhearless enters to Ranger McPhearless's theme song.)

RANGER MCPHEARLESS: Adventure calls! *("Woo-hoo!")* Ah-ha! I'm glad you're both awake. I have a surprise for you.

QUINT AND MIMI: What is it?

RANGER MCPHEARLESS: I found someone going back to the city. They can take you with them if you want to go, but you'll have to hurry. They can only wait a few more minutes.

MIMI: Thank you, Ranger McPhearless, but I think I'll stay.

QUINT: Really?

MIMI: Yeah.

QUINT: Are we roasting marshmallows again tonight?

RANGER MCPHEARLESS: Yes.

QUINT: Then I'll stay too.

RANGER MCPHEARLESS: *(Taken aback)* I can't believe it. You've complained all week that you want to go home. And now you don't. You two are unpredictable.

QUINT: It's an eye-opener for me too.

RANGER MCPHEARLESS: That reminds me of what we're learning about God today.

MIMI: What do you mean?

RANGER MCPHEARLESS: Well, God is unpredictable too.

QUINT: Hold on a second. What do you mean, God is unpredictable? I thought God was unchanging and trustworthy and true?

RANGER MCPHEARLESS: He is. We can always trust God—he doesn't change who he is. He is always good and loving and true.

MIMI: Then how is he unpredictable?

RANGER MCPHEARLESS: God did lots of surprising things in the Bible that were different than what people expected. And he leads us down unexpected and awesome paths every day.

QUINT: Really?

MIMI: I guess he can do anything because he is God.

RANGER MCPHEARLESS: He knows the right thing to do, even when people don't. In the Old Testament, God appeared to the prophet Elijah and was completely unpredictable. It's a pretty cool story—with wind and fire and earthquakes.

QUINT: Sounds dangerous.

MIMI: And exciting.

RANGER MCPHEARLESS: If you're staying, you'll find out more about it.

MIMI: We'll be here.

RANGER MCPHEARLESS: Then I'll see you with the Adventurers later. I'd better go tell the people that are leaving that you won't be joining them. Adventure calls! *("Woo-hoo!")*

(Ranger McPhearless exits.)

MIMI: Wow. That was a sudden turn of events. I'm glad I'm staying.

QUINT: Since we are staying, let's join the Adventurers and find out more about how God is unpredictable.

(Mimi and Quint exit.)

Bible Story
The Birth of Jesus
(Luke 2:1–20;
Matthew 2:1–12)

Key Verse
And we have seen and testify that the Father has sent his Son to be the Savior of the world.
(1 John 4:14)

Live It!
God is unforgettable.

Script Day 5

Cast:
• Ranger McPhearless, Quint, and Mimi. Both Quint and Mimi now have dirt smudges on their faces and clothing. They also have twigs and leaves stuck in their hair. Mimi's hair has tangles in it.

Props:
• Glass jar with lid and a bug inside; Ranger McPhearless's theme music.

RANGER RILEY: Adventurers, let's welcome Ranger McPhearless. Come on up here, Ranger McPhearless.

(Ranger Riley exits the stage as Ranger McPhearless enters to the theme music.)

RANGER MCPHEARLESS: Hi, everybody. Adventure calls! *("Woo-hoo!")* Hasn't this been a great week in Wildwood Forest?

(As children yell their answers, Quint and Mimi walk onstage, talking and laughing together. They are covered with dirt, twigs, and sticks, but seem oblivious to it. Ranger McPhearless sees them.)

RANGER MCPHEARLESS: Hi, Quint and Mimi. Wow! You sure look … different …

QUINT: Oh, hi, Ranger McPhearless. Sorry we're late.

MIMI: We've had a very busy morning.

RANGER MCPHEARLESS: What have you been doing?

QUINT: Oh, not much … we were hungry, so we decided to climb up a gigantic birch tree, remove a huge beehive, cut it open, and eat the honey.

RANGER MCPHEARLESS: You did what? *(Elbowing Quint with a wink)* But that's dangerous.

MIMI: Don't worry. Quint researched how to do it so that no one would get hurt.

QUINT: And then we wanted some exercise, so we went hiking and found a lake and went for a swim.

MIMI: There were some really big fish in it … and it was very cold …

QUINT: But it was exhilarating.

MIMI: Then we saw a wild moose …

QUINT: He was about ten feet tall …

MIMI: So we hopped on his back …

QUINT: … and went for a ride.

MIMI: After that we were kind of tired …

QUINT: So we built a shelter out of logs and took a quick nap.

MIMI: After our nap, we were hungry so we picked some wild berries …

QUINT: And fashioned a canoe from a log so we could go for a canoe ride …

MIMI: And Quint caught some fish in the river with his bare hands …

QUINT: And then Mimi found an amazing insect and caught it in a jar …

(Mimi proudly holds out a glass jar for Ranger McPhearless to see.)

MIMI: So that's why we're a bit late.

RANGER MCPHEARLESS: I can't believe you did all that this morning!

(Quint and Mimi laugh.)

QUINT: We're just kidding. We caught this amazing insect this morning. That's all.

MIMI: But the other things are what we put on a list to try sometime.

RANGER MCPHEARLESS: Quite a change from the nervous cityfolk you were when you came here. Adventure calls! ("*Woo-hoo!*")

(*Quint and Mimi join the "woo-hoo!" enthusiastically.*)

QUINT: Sure, Ranger McPhearless, at first we were a little … uncomfortable … with Wildwood Forest. But once Mimi convinced me to try some new things, well, I love it here.

MIMI: So do I. Our experience has been unforgettable.

QUINT: We learned that God is undefeatable and unmatchable.

MIMI: And he's uncontainable and unpredictable.

QUINT: And we've had adventures and new experiences here we'll never forget.

MIMI: And made friends we'll never forget.

QUINT: I can't believe the week is over already …

MIMI: I can't believe it either …

RANGER MCPHEARLESS: Wait a minute. Wipe those sad looks off your faces. The week isn't over. We've got one more day! And this is going to be the most unforgettable day of all in Wildwood Forest.

QUINT: It is?

RANGER MCPHEARLESS: Yesiree! Today we're going to learn about God's wild love for us and how he showed us that love in an awesome way. He came to be one of us. He came to be our Savior.

QUINT: Are we going to explore the story of Jesus' birth?

RANGER MCPHEARLESS: That's right!

QUINT: I can't wait.

MIMI: Me either.

RANGER MCPHEARLESS: Well, come on, guys! Adventure calls! ("*Woo-hoo!*")

(*Ranger McPhearless bounds energetically offstage. Quint and Mimi slowly follow, talking as they go.*)

MIMI: This has been the most unforgettable week of my life.

QUINT: Mine too. But do you know what the most unforgettable part of all is?

MIMI: What?

QUINT: God.

(*They all exit.*)

Day 5 Closing Program Script

Closing Assembly Skit

Cast:
- Ranger McPhearless, Quint, and Mimi. Quint and Mimi still have dirt smudged on their faces and clothing. They also have twigs and leaves stuck in their hair. Mimi's hair, in particular, should look completely wild, tangled and messy.

Props:
- Mimi's blow dryer, curling iron, and hairbrush, along with Quint and Mimi's other outdoor equipment (backpacks, sleeping bags, bug spray, etc.), scattered all over the stage; Ranger McPhearless's theme music.

RANGER RILEY: Well, how do you think Quint and Mimi ended their last day at Wildwood Forest? Let's see.

(Quint and Mimi enter. They begin to pack all the scattered equipment, piece by piece.)

MIMI: I can't believe the week is over, Quint.

QUINT: I know what you mean, Mimi.

MIMI: I don't know if I really want to go back ... to city life.

QUINT: This week has changed what's important to me.

MIMI: I'm not the same girl I used to be.

QUINT: Your hairdo has certainly changed.

MIMI: Why did I bring so much stuff? I'm not sure I ever want to use any of this stuff again.

QUINT: Well, don't take it too far. I mean, there's nothing wrong with combing your hair and washing your face every day.

MIMI: You know what I mean.

QUINT: I do know what you mean. I've changed too, Mimi. I used to be such a ... a coward. I didn't want any adventure in my life. I never wanted any risk. I just wanted to be in control all the time.

MIMI: This week, we both realized that God is the one who's in control.

QUINT: And ... well ... I was really missing out on all the excitement, the way I used to live. I don't want to leave Wildwood Forest now.

MIMI: Me either, Quint ... me either.

(Ranger McPhearless enters to his theme music.)

RANGER MCPHEARLESS: Adventure calls! *("Woo-hoo!")*

(Looks around as Quint and Mimi don't respond with "woo-hoo!") **What's the matter? Why the long faces?**

QUINT AND MIMI: We don't want to go home.

RANGER MCPHEARLESS: I know it's hard to leave Wildwood Forest …

QUINT: It's so exciting here.

MIMI: And beautiful.

QUINT: And God is here.

RANGER MCPHEARLESS: Whoa, there! Wildwood Forest is awesome. It's a place unlike any other. And it's been a great, amazing, unbelievable week. But God isn't just here. He's everywhere.

MIMI: Really? God will be with us when we go back to city life?

RANGER MCPHEARLESS: Sure will! And the beauty of God's creation will still be there too—just look up at the stars at night. You'll be amazed at what you see.

QUINT: But this faith adventure has been amazing.

RANGER MCPHEARLESS: Growing in your faith doesn't have to end when you leave Wildwood Forest. The rest of your life can be an adventure with God, if you choose to follow him daily.

MIMI: So every single day—every single moment—can be filled with trust and hope and faith in our amazing God?

RANGER MCPHEARLESS: God is undefeatable, unmatchable, uncontainable, unpredictable, and unforgettable. That's true no matter where you are.

MIMI: That's great! It means we can be on an adventure every day of our lives no matter where we live.

QUINT: Then I'm not going back to the way I used to live.

MIMI: Me neither.

RANGER MCPHERSON: Good idea. Live every day the way you're meant to—as a real adventure with God. Adventure calls! *("Woo-hoo!")*

(The three pick up the bags and head offstage. Ranger McPhearless, Quint, and Mimi exit the stage.)